THEFT, BURGLARY, & ROBBERY IN OKLAHOMA

Offenses, Penalties, & Defenses

Don't panic!
Call Urbanic.™

Frank A. Urbanic, Esq.

ISBN: 978-1-946481-11-5

Designed and Published by:

Speakeasy Publications
73-03 Bell Blvd, #10
Oakland Gardens, NY 11364
www.SpeakeasyMarketingInc.com
888-225-8594

DISCLAIMER

This publication is intended to be informational only. No legal advice is being given, and no attorney-client relationship is intended to be created by reading this material. If you are facing legal issues, whether criminal or civil, seek professional legal counsel to get your questions answered. The law cited is current as of November 1, 2017. Laws are subject to change at any time.

THE URBANIC LAW FIRM, PLLC

1141 N Robinson Avenue
Suite 101
Oklahoma City, OK 73103
(405) 633-3420

Frank@Urbanic.Law

www.Urbanic.Law

Table Of Contents

About Frank Urbanic

I became a criminal defense attorney because I'm intimately familiar with how precious our constitutional rights are. After my arrest years ago, I realized how close I was to being in a situation that could have negatively impacted my life forever. That

experience made me realize how important it is to have someone on your side who feels strongly about protecting your rights.

In the Air Force, I put my life on the line to support and defend the Constitution during combat. Today, I support and defend the Constitution in the courtroom. My legal career began by representing indigent clients. I saw first-hand how important it is for everyone to have legal representation.

Through my extensive business training at The University of Oklahoma and Texas A&M University, I've learned proven business techniques that allow me to operate a lean and efficient law firm. These techniques include document automation, checklists, templates, the use of cutting-edge technology, and continuous process improvement practices. My firm uses these business techniques to produce high-quality legal representation in a fraction of the time. Less waste means more value to my clients.

While many offices are still dealing with paper folders, we are digital. No missing documents. No messy folders. Using cloud-based technology, I can work on your case from anywhere on the planet. Whether I'm in a Starbucks or in an airplane at 30,000 ft, I'm still able to work on cases.

What Makes My Firm Suited To Defend Your Rights

- Extensive Experience In Handling Criminal Defense Cases
- Rated Superb On AVVO.com
- Employing Cutting-Edge Technology To The Benefit Of Our Clients
- Providing High-Quality Criminal Defense At A Reasonable Price
- Intensive Criminal Defense Training In The Caprock Regional Public Defender Office

My Firm Has Handled Cases In The Following Areas

- Criminal Defense
- DUI, DWI, & APC
- Domestic Assault & Battery
- Theft Crimes
- Drug Possession, Distribution, and Trafficking
- Traffic Tickets

Additional Training

- Standardized Field Sobriety Test (SFST) Instructor
- Standardized Field Sobriety Test (SFST) Practitioner
- Advanced Roadside Impaired Driving Enforcement (ARIDE) Practitioner
- Drug Recognition Expert (DRE) Overview Course graduate
- Oklahoma State Bureau of Investigation Forensics Academy graduate

Professional Associations And Memberships

- National Association of Criminal Defense Lawyers
- National College for DUI Defense
- Oklahoma Criminal Defense Lawyers Association
- Oklahoma Bar Association
- Oklahoma County Bar Association
- Canadian County Bar Association
- Oklahoma County Criminal Defense Lawyers Association

- Order of the Coif
- Phi Kappa Phi

Books

- Oklahoma DUI Survival Guide
- Oklahoma Drug Laws
- Domestic Violence & Victim Protective Orders In Oklahoma

Bar Admissions

- Oklahoma

INTRODUCTION

This book was published in November 2017. Oklahoma has made many changes to theft laws in the year preceding the publication of this book. The laws referenced are those in effect on November 1, 2017. The most recent changes to these laws went into effect on July 1, 2017 due to State Question (SQ) 780.

The law that applies to a charge is the law that was in effect on the date the offense occurred. If an offense occurred prior to July 1, 2017, then the most accurate law can be found by viewing the superseded document linked at the bottom of the statute on the Oklahoma State Court Network (OSCN) website. There are continuing efforts to enact further changes to Oklahoma's property crime laws. If a change occurs after the publication of this book, then the most accurate statute will be found on OSCN.

Oklahoma has numerous laws covering theft, burglary, and robbery. It would be impractical to list them all in this book. I have chosen to discuss the most frequently charged crimes in those areas. Additionally, this book discusses some fairly obscure theft laws because it includes every theft crime modified by SQ 780.

WHAT IS THEFT IN OKLAHOMA?

Oklahoma still uses many of the common law definitions of theft, such as larceny, false pretenses (fraud), shoplifting, and embezzlement. There are different technical definitions for each even though they all fall under the umbrella of theft. Receiving stolen property is also in the category of theft crimes.

The primary theft crime is larceny. It is defined in 21 O.S. § 1701 as the taking the personal property of another by stealth or fraud and with the intent to deprive another thereof. Larceny is divided into two degrees—Grand Larceny and Petit Larceny.

Petit Larceny

Petit Larceny occurs when the value of the property taken is equal to or less than $1,000 and the property was not taken from the person of another. The maximum punishment in the county jail is six months. The range of fine is $10–$500.

Grand Larceny

Grand Larceny occurs when the value of the property taken exceeds $1,000 or when the property, although worth less than $1,000, is taken from the person of another. Grand larceny is a felony. The maximum punishment in the Department of Corrections is five years if the value of the property is $1,000 or more. If the value of the property is less than $1,000, it is punishable by incarceration in the county jail for up to one year or by incarceration in the county jail one or more nights or weekends. The maximum fine is $5,000. Restitution must be paid. Voters approved a change to this statute on November 8, 2017 by passing State Question 780. The change went into effect on July 1, 2017.

SOURCES: 21 O.S. § 1701, 21 O.S. § 1704, 21 O.S. § 1705, & 21 O.S. § 1706

Other Larceny Crimes

There are other larceny crimes that depend on the facts surrounding the incident. These are Larceny of Property Taken From the Person, Larceny From Person at Night, Grand Larceny in Dwelling House, and Larceny From Building.

Larceny Of Property Taken From The Person

Grand Larceny occurs when property is taken from the person of another. The value of the property does not matter. The maximum punishment in the Department of Corrections is five years if the value of the property is $1,000 or more. If the value of the property is less than $1,000, it is punishable by incarceration in the county jail for not more than one year or by incarceration in the county jail one or more nights or weekends. The maximum fine is $5,000. Restitution must be paid. Voters approved a change to this statute on November 8, 2017 by passing State Question 780. The change went into effect on July 1, 2017.

SOURCE: 21 O.S. § 1704

Larceny From Person At Night

Larceny committed by stealing in the nighttime from the person of another is a felony. The maximum punishment in the Department of Corrections is ten years. The maximum fine is $5,000. Restitution must be paid.

SOURCE: 21 O.S. § 1708

Grand Larceny In Dwelling House

Grand Larceny committed in any dwelling house or vessel is a felony. The maximum punishment in the Department of Corrections is eight years. A "vessel," when used with reference to shipping, includes ships of all kinds, steamboats, and steamships, canal boats, and every structure adapted to be navigated from place to place.

SOURCES: 21 O.S. § 1707 & 21 O.S. § 98

Larceny From Building

Entering and stealing any money or other thing of value from any house, railroad car, tent, booth, or temporary building is a felony. The maximum punishment in the Department of Corrections is five years.

SOURCES: 21 O.S. § 1723 & 21 O.S. § 1724

Lost Property

It is considered larceny to find lost property under circumstances that give you knowledge or means of inquiry as to the true owner if you appropriate the property to your own use, or to the use of another person who is not entitled to the property, without having first made an effort to find the owner and restore the property to the rightful owner as the circumstances render reasonable and just.

SOURCE: 21 O.S. § 1702

Oklahoma has numerous theft crimes that focus on specific actions or property. Some of these are: False Declaration of Ownership to a Pawnbroker; Taking Oil, Gas, or Gasoline; Theft of Cable or Telecommunications Service; Larceny of Dog, Sheep, Goat, Horse, Jackass, Jennet, Mule, Cow, Hog, or Implement of Husbandry; Larceny of Domestic Fowl; Unlawfully Possessing a Stray Animal; and Larceny of Domesticated Fish and Game.

False Declaration Of Ownership To A Pawnbroker

Selling or pledging property to a pawnbroker using false or altered identification or a false declaration of ownership violates 59 O.S. § 1512. It is a felony if the value of the property is $1,000 or more. The maximum punishment in the Department of Corrections is five years, and the maximum punishment in the county jail is one year. The maximum fine is $500.

If the property was acquired by means of robbery or

burglary, the maximum punishment in the Department of Corrections is five years, and the maximum punishment in the county jail is one year. The maximum fine is $500. The value of the property does not matter.

It is a misdemeanor to fail to repay a pawnbroker the full amount received from a pawn or buy transaction after being officially notified by a peace officer that the goods pledged or sold in that transaction were stolen or embezzled. The maximum punishment in the county jail is six months. The maximum fine is $500. Voters approved a change to this statute on November 8, 2017 by passing SQ 780. The change went into effect on July 1, 2017.

SOURCE: 59 O.S. § 1512

Taking Oil, Gas, or Gasoline

It is a violation of 21 O.S. § 1722 to unlawfully take any crude oil or gasoline, or any product thereof, from any pipe, pipeline, tank, tank car, or other receptacle or container. It is also a crime to unlawfully take or cause to be taken any machinery, drilling mud, equipment, or other materials necessary for the drilling or production of oil or gas wells, with intent to deprive the owner or lessee thereof of that crude oil, gas, gasoline, or any product thereof, machinery, drilling mud, equipment, or other materials necessary for the drilling or production of oil or gas wells.

This crime is a misdemeanor if the value of the above-mentioned product is less than $1,000. The maximum punishment in the county jail is 60 days. The maximum fine is $500. This crime is a felony if the value of the above-mentioned product is $1,000 or more. The range of punishment in the Department of Corrections is one–ten years. The range of fine is $100–$50,000. Voters approved a change to this statute on November 8, 2017 by passing State Question 780. The change went into effect on July 1, 2017.

SOURCE: 21 O.S. § 1722

Theft Of Cable Or Telecommunications Service

It is illegal to:

1. knowingly obtain or attempt to obtain cable, information, or telecommunications service of any type or kind including but not limited to cable television, telephony, internet, and data transmission service from another by means, artifice, trick, deception, or

device without the payment to the operator of said service of all lawful compensation for each type of service obtained;

2. knowingly assist or instruct any other person in obtaining or attempting to obtain cable, information, or telecommunications service of any type or kind including, but not limited to, cable television, telephony, internet, and data transmission service without the payment to the operator of all lawful compensations;

3. knowingly tamper or otherwise interfere with or connect to by any means, whether mechanical, electrical, acoustical, or other means, any cables, wires, or other devices used for the distribution of cable, information, or telecommunications service of any type or kind including but not limited to cable television, telephony, internet, and data transmission service without authority from the operator of said service; or

4. knowingly manufacture, import into Oklahoma, distribute, sell, offer for sale, rental, or use, possess for sale, rental, or use, or advertise for sale, rental, or use any device of any description, or any plan, or kit for a device, designed in whole or in part to facilitate the doing of any of the acts specified in the above paragraphs.

The existence on the property and in the actual possession of the accused, of: 1) any connection, wire, conductor, or any device whatsoever, which is connected in such a manner as would appear to permit the use of cable, information, or telecommunications service of any type or kind including, but not limited to, cable television, telephony, internet, and data transmission service without the same being reported for payment to and specifically authorized by the operator of the cable, information, or telecommunications service of any type or kind including but not limited to cable television, telephony, internet, and data transmission service or 2) the existence on the property and in the actual possession of the accused, in quantities or volumes suggesting possession for resale, of any device designed in whole or in part to facilitate the performance of any of the illegal acts mentioned in this statute will be prima facie evidence of intent to violate and of the violation of the provisions of this law.

This crime is a misdemeanor. The maximum punishment in the county jail is six months. The maximum fine is $1,000.

Any person who violates this law is liable to the franchised or otherwise duly licensed cable television system, information service provider, or other telecommunications service or equipment provider for the greater of the following amounts: 1) $2,500 or 2) three times the amount of actual damages, if any, sustained by the plaintiff, plus reasonable attorney's fees.

Any franchised or otherwise duly licensed cable television system, information service provider, or other telecommunications service or equipment provider may bring an action to enjoin and restrain any violation of this law or an action of conversion, or both, and may in the same action seek damages as provided for above. It's not a necessary prerequisite to an action pursuant to this law that the plaintiff has suffered, or be threatened with, actual damages.

SOURCE: 21 O.S. § 1737

Larceny Of Dog, Sheep, Goat, Horse, Jackass, Jennet, Mule, Cow, Hog, Or Implement Of Husbandry

All dogs are considered the personal property of their owner for all purposes. The taking of dogs is considered larceny. It is punishable in the same manner and to the same degree as in larceny of other personal property.

It is a felony to steal any dog, sheep, or goat. The range of punishment in the Department of Corrections is six months–three years. The maximum fine is up to three times the value of the animals that were stolen but not more than $500,000.

It is a felony to steal any horse, jackass, jennet, mule, cow, hog, or implement of husbandry. The range of punishment in the Department of Corrections is three–ten years. The maximum fine is three times the value of animals and machinery that were stolen but not more than $500,000. Each head of cattle stolen may constitute a separate offense and may be punishable as a separate violation.

The word "horse" includes all animals of the equine species, and the word "cow" includes all animals of the bovine species.

With regards to implements of husbandry, every device, whether it is self-propelled, designed and adapted to be used exclusively for agricultural, horticultural or livestock-raising operations or for lifting or carrying an implement of husbandry and, in either case, not subject to registration if operated upon the highways. Implements of husbandry are as follows:

- farm wagon type tank trailers of not over 1,200 gallons

capacity, used during the liquid fertilizer season as field storage "nurse tanks" supplying the fertilizer to a field applicator and moved on highways only for bringing the fertilizer from a local source of supply to farms or field or from one farm or field to another;

- trailers or semitrailers (except for those with an axle weight of 20,000 pounds or more, which is used to haul manure and operated on the public roads or highways) owned by a person engaged in the business of farming and used exclusively for transporting farm products to market or for the purpose of transporting to the farm material or things to be used thereon;

- utility-type, all-terrain vehicles with a maximum curb weight of 1,500 pounds that are equipped with metal front or rear carrying racks when used for agricultural, horticultural or livestock-raising operations.

SOURCES: 21 O.S. § 1718, 21 O.S. § 1717, 21 O.S. § 1716, & 47 O.S. §1-125

Larceny Of Domestic Fowl

Per 21 O.S. § 1719, it is grand larceny to steal and carry away domestic fowl or receive domestic fowl knowing the fowl to be stolen. The value of the fowl(s) doesn't matter. The maximum punishment in the Department of Corrections is five years. The maximum punishment in the county jail is two months. The maximum fine is $200.

SOURCE: 21 O.S. § 1719

Unlawfully Possessing A Stray Animal

According to 4 O.S. § 85.11, it's illegal to take in and keep a stray animal without first making a reasonable investigation to ascertain the animal's owner. The taker must report this taking to the county sheriff within seven days.

Violation of this law is a felony. If the stray is a dog, sheep, or goat, the range of punishment in the Department of Corrections is six months–three years. The maximum fine is up to three times the value of the animals that were kept but not more than $500,000.

If the stray is a horse, jackass, jennet, mule, cow, or hog, the range of punishment in the Department of Corrections is three–ten years. The maximum fine is three times the value of animals that were kept but not more than $500,000. Each head of cattle kept may constitute a separate offense and may be punishable as a separate violation.

SOURCES: 4 O.S. § 85.3, 4 O.S. § 85.11, & 21 O.S. § 1716

Larceny Of Domesticated Fish And Game

Domesticated fish or game is defined as all birds, mammals, fish, and other aquatic forms and all other animals, regardless of classifications, whether resident, migratory or imported, protected or unprotected, dead or alive. The definition extends to and includes every part of any individual species when such domesticated fish or game are not in the wild and are in the possession of a person currently licensed to possess such fish or game. “Taking" means the pursuing, killing, capturing, trapping, snaring and netting of domesticated fish or game or placing, setting, drawing or using any net, trap or other device for taking domesticated fish or game and includes specifically every attempt to take such domesticated fish or game. Any domesticated fish or game shall be considered the personal property of the owner.

It’s a crime to take any domesticated fish or game with the intent to deprive the owner of said fish or game. This crime is a misdemeanor if the current market value of the domesticated fish or game is less than $1,000. The maximum punishment in the county jail is 60 days. The maximum fine is $500. This crime is a felony if the current market value of stolen domesticated fish or game is $1,000 or more. The maximum punishment in the Department of Corrections is five years. Voters approved a change to this statute on November 8, 2017 by passing State Question 780. The change went into effect on July 1, 2017.

SOURCE: 21 O.S. § 1719.1

FORGERY

Forgery in the third degree occurs when a person:

1. who, with intent to defraud, has in his or her possession any forged, altered or counterfeit negotiable note, bill, draft or other evidence of debt issued or purporting to have been issued by any corporation or company duly authorized for that purpose by the laws of Oklahoma or of any other state, government or country, knowing the same to be forged, altered or counterfeited, with intent to utter the same as true or as false, or to cause the same to be so uttered;
2. sells, exchanges or delivers for any consideration any forged or counterfeited promissory note, check, bill, draft, or other evidence of debt, or engagement for the payment of money absolutely, or upon any contingency, knowing the same to be forged or counterfeited, with intent to have the same uttered or passed, or who offers any such note or other instrument for sale, exchange or delivery for any consideration, with the like knowledge and intent, or who receives any such note or other instrument upon a sale, exchange or delivery for any consideration with the like knowledge and intent; or
3. has in his possession any forged or counterfeited instrument, knowing the same to be forged, counterfeited or falsely altered with intent to injure or defraud by uttering the same to be true, or as false, or by causing the same to be uttered.

This crime is a misdemeanor if the value of the forgery is less than $1,000. The maximum punishment in the county jail is one year, and the maximum fine is $1,000. This crime is a felony if the value of the forgery is $1,000 or more; the maximum punishment in the Department of Corrections is seven years. If the total or aggregate value of the forgery is $2,000 or more, the maximum punishment in the Department of Corrections is seven years. Voters approved a change to this statute on November 8, 2017 by passing State Question 780. The change went into effect on July 1, 2017.

SOURCES: 21 O.S. § 1577, 21 O.S. § 1578, 21 O.S. § 1579, & 21 O.S. § 1621

False Pretenses, Deception, or Trick

This category of offenses includes False Pretenses; Obtaining Property by Trick or Deception; and False or Bogus Checks, Drafts, or Orders

False Pretenses

False pretenses in Oklahoma is defined in 21 O.S. § 1542. It is the obtaining from any person any money or property or obtaining the signature of any person to any written instrument with the intent to cheat or defraud another, designedly, by color or aid of any false token or writing, or other false pretense.

This crime is a misdemeanor if the value of the money or property obtained is less than $1,000. The maximum punishment in the county jail is one year. The maximum fine is three times the value of the money or property obtained.

This crime is a felony if the value of the money or property is $1,000 or more. The maximum punishment is three years in the Department of Corrections or one year in a county jail. The maximum fine is three times the value of the money or property obtained.

SOURCE: 21 O.S. § 1542

Obtaining Property By Trick Or Deception

It is illegal to obtain or attempt to obtain any money, property, or valuable thing from any person, firm, or corporation with intent to cheat and defraud by means or by use of any trick or deception, or false or fraudulent representation or statement or pretense, or by any other means or instruments or device commonly called the "confidence game," or by means or use of any false or bogus checks, or by any other written or printed or engraved instrument or spurious coin.

This crime is a misdemeanor if the value of the property obtained is less than $1,000. The maximum punishment in the county jail is one year, and the maximum fine is $1,000.

This crime is a felony if the value of the property obtained is $1,000 or more. The maximum punishment in the Department of Corrections is ten years, and the maximum fine is $5,000. Voters approved a change to this statute on November 8, 2017 by passing State Question 780. The change went into effect on July 1, 2017.

SOURCES: 21 O.S. § 1541.1 & 21 O.S. § 1541.2

False Or Bogus Checks, Drafts, Or Orders

It's illegal to make, draw, utter, or deliver two or more false or bogus checks, drafts, or orders. "False or bogus check or checks" includes checks or orders, including those converted to electronic fund transfer, which are not honored on account of insufficient funds of the maker to pay same or because the check or order was drawn on a closed account or on a nonexistent account when such checks or orders are given:

1. in exchange for money or property;
2. in exchange for any benefit or thing of value;
3. as a down payment for the purchase of any item of which the purchaser is taking immediate possession, as against the maker or drawer thereof; or
4. as payment made to a landlord under a lease or rental agreement.

The making, drawing, uttering, or delivering of a check, draft, or order, payment of which is refused by the drawee, is prima facie evidence of intent to defraud and the knowledge of insufficient funds in, or credit with, such bank or other depository; provided, such maker or drawer shall not have paid the drawee thereof the amount due thereon, together with the protest fees, within five days from the date the same is presented for payment; and provided, further, that the check or order is presented for payment within 30 days after same is delivered and accepted. A check offered for the purchase of goods or livestock that is refused by a drawee will not be considered to be an extension of credit by the seller of goods or livestock to the maker or drawer of the check. A check or order offered to a merchant in payment on an open account of the maker with the merchant means "a check or order given in exchange for a benefit or thing of value," notwithstanding that the merchant may debit the account of the maker or impose other charges pursuant to applicable law in the event the check or order is not honored.

This crime is a felony if the total sum of the false or bogus checks, drafts, or orders is $1,000 or more even though each separate instrument is written for less than $1,000—

so long as all were written in pursuance of a common scheme or plan to cheat and defraud. The maximum punishment in the Department of Corrections is ten years, and the maximum fine is $5,000. Voters approved a change to this statute on November 8, 2017 by passing State Question 780. The change went into effect on July 1, 2017.

SOURCES: 21 O.S. § 1541.3 & 21 O.S. § 1541.4

The general fraud statute is 15 O.S. § 58. It consists of the following acts, committed by a party to a contract, or with his or her connivance, with the intent to deceive another party to the contract, or to induce that party to enter into the contract:

1. the suggestion, as a fact, of that which is not true, by one who does not believe it to be true;
2. the positive assertion in a manner not warranted by the information of the person making it, of that which is not true, though he believes it to be true;
3. the suppression of that which is true, by one having knowledge or belief of the fact;
4. a promise made without any intention of performing it; or
5. any other act fitted to deceive.

SOURCE: 15 O.S. § 58

Oklahoma has numerous crimes that fall under the umbrella of "fraud." Two of the most common are Fraudulent Vehicle Lease or Rental by Bogus Check and Defrauding Hotels, Inns, Restaurants, Etc.

Fraudulent Vehicle Lease Or Rental By Bogus Check

Leasing or renting any motor vehicle with the intent to cheat and defraud while paying the fees for such lease or rental by means of a false, bogus, or worthless check violates 21 O.S. § 152. This crime is a misdemeanor if the value of the check is less than $1,000. The maximum punishment in the county jail is six months, and the maximum fine is $500. This crime is a felony if the value of the worthless check is $1,000 or more. The maximum punishment in the Department of Corrections is seven years, and the maximum fine is $500. Voters approved a change to this statute on November 8, 2017 by passing State Question 780. The change went into effect on July 1, 2017.

SOURCE: 21 O.S. § 1521

Defrauding Innkeeper, Hotel, Restaurant, etc.

Obtaining food, lodging, services, or other accommodations at any hotel, inn, restaurant, boarding house, rooming house, motel, or auto camp with intent to defraud the owner or keeper violates 21 O.S. § 1503. This crime is a misdemeanor if the value of the food, lodging, services, or other accommodations is less than $1,000.

The maximum fine is $500. The maximum punishment in county jail is three months. This crime is a felony if the value of the food, lodging, services, or accommodations is $1,000 or more. The maximum punishment in the Department of Corrections is five years.

It's a misdemeanor to obtain shelter, lodging, or any other services at any apartment house, apartment, rental unit, rental house, or trailer camp, with intent to defraud the owner or keeper thereof. The maximum fine is $100. The maximum punishment in the county jail is three months.

Prima facie proof of the intent to defraud occurs when proof that such lodging, food, services, or other accommodations were obtained by false pretense or by false or fictitious show or pretense of any baggage or other property, or giving a check on which payment was refused, or leaving the hotel, inn, restaurant, boarding house, rooming house, motel, apartment house, apartment, rental unit or rental house, trailer camp, or auto camp, without payment or offering to pay for such food, lodging, services or other accommodation, or surreptitiously removing or attempting to remove baggage, or registering under a fictitious name. This statute does not apply where there has been an agreement in writing for delay in payment. Voters approved a change to this statute on November 8, 2017 by passing State Question 780. The change went into effect on July 1, 2017.

SOURCE: 21 O.S. § 1503

EMBEZZLEMENT

Embezzlement in Oklahoma is defined in 21 O.S. § 1451. It is the fraudulent appropriation of property of any person or legal entity, legally obtained, to any use or purpose not intended or authorized by its owner, or the secretion of the property with the fraudulent intent to appropriate it to such use or purpose where:

- the property was obtained by being entrusted to that person for a specific purpose, use, or disposition and shall include, but not be limited to, any funds "held in trust" for any purpose;
- the property was obtained by virtue of a power of attorney being granted for the sale or transfer of the property;
- the property is possessed or controlled for the use of another person;
- the property is to be used for a public or benevolent purpose;
- any person diverts any money appropriated by law from the purpose and object of the appropriation;
- any person fails or refuses to pay over to the state, or appropriate authority, any tax or other monies

collected in accordance with state law, and who appropriates the tax or monies to the use of that person, or to the use of any other person not entitled to the tax or monies;

- the property is possessed for the purpose of transportation, without regard to whether packages containing the property have been broken;
- any person removes crops from any leased or rented premises with the intent to deprive the owner or landlord interested in the land of any of the rent due from that land, or who fraudulently appropriates the rent to that person or any other person; or
- the property is possessed or controlled by virtue of a lease or rental agreement, and the property is willfully or intentionally not returned within ten days after the expiration of the agreement.

Punishment For An Embezzlement Conviction

This crime is a misdemeanor if the value of the property embezzled is less than $1,000. The maximum fine is $1,000. The maximum punishment in the county jail is one year.

This crime is a felony if the value of the property embezzled is $1,000 or more. If the value of the property is greater than or equal $1,000 but less than $25,000, the maximum punishment in the Department of Corrections is five years. The maximum fine is $5,000. Restitution must be paid.

If the value of the property embezzled is $25,000 or more, the maximum punishment in the Department of Corrections is ten years, and the maximum fine is $10,000. Restitution must be paid.

A series of offenses may be aggregated into one offense when they are the result of the formulation of a plan, scheme, or the setting up of a mechanism which, when put into operation, results in the taking or diversion of money or property on a recurring basis. When all acts result from a continuing course of conduct, they may be aggregated into one crime. Acts forming an integral part of the first taking that facilitate subsequent takings, or acts taken in preparation of several takings that facilitate subsequent takings, are relevant to determine the party's intent to commit a continuing crime. Voters approved a change to this statute on November 8, 2017 by passing State Question 780. The change went into effect on July 1, 2017.

SOURCE: 21 O.S. § 1451

RECEIVING OR CONCEALING STOLEN PROPERTY

Receiving or concealing stolen property is defined in 21 O.S. § 1713. It occurs when someone buys or receives, in any manner, upon any consideration, any personal property of any value whatsoever that has been stolen, embezzled, or obtained by false pretense or robbery. The recipient must know or have reasonable cause to believe the property to have been stolen, embezzled, or obtained by false pretense or robbery—or the person conceals, withholds, or aids in concealing or withholding such property from the owner.

The statute uses a reasonable person standard to determine if you received stolen property under such circumstances that would cause you to believe that the property was indeed stolen. If you, without making reasonable inquiry, buy, receive, conceal, withhold, or aid in concealing or withholding any property that has been stolen, embezzled, or obtained by false pretense or robbery, or otherwise feloniously obtained, under such circumstances as should cause such person to make reasonable inquiry to ascertain that the person from whom such property was bought or received had the legal right to sell or deliver it will be presumed to have bought or received such property knowing it to have been stolen or wrongfully obtained. This presumption may, however, be rebutted by proof.

The statute relies upon the belief that a reasonable person would make an inquiry to ascertain from whom the property was bought or received and if that individual had a legal right to sell or deliver it. If these questions cannot be answered, the law presumes that the individual who bought or received such property knew it to be stolen or unlawfully obtained. In other words, even if somebody received stolen property and did not know that it was stolen but the circumstances surrounding it were so fishy that a reasonable person would have asked to find out if it was stolen, then that individual can still be found guilty of receiving stolen property.

Punishment For Receiving Or Concealing Stolen Property

This crime is a misdemeanor if the value of the property is less than $1,000. The maximum fine is $500, and the maximum punishment in the county jail is six months.

This crime is a felony if the value of the property is $1,000 or more. The maximum punishment in the Department of Corrections is five years, and the maximum punishment in the county jail is one year. The maximum fine is $500. Voters approved a change to this statute on November 8, 2017 by passing State Question 780. The change went into effect on July 1, 2017.

SOURCE: 21 O.S. § 1713

SHOPLIFTING

Shoplifting in Oklahoma is defined in 21 O.S. § 1731 as the larceny of merchandise held for sale in retail or wholesale establishments.

Punishment for Shoplifting in Oklahoma

The first or second shoplifting conviction is a misdemeanor if the value of shoplifted items is less than $1,000. The maximum punishment in the county jail is 30 days. The fine range is $10–$500. If more than one item has been taken in the first or second conviction, then the minimum fine increases to $50.

If it is shown, in the trial of a case in which the value of the shoplifted property is less than $1,000, that the defendant has been convicted of shoplifting two or more times, then, on a third or subsequent conviction, the maximum punishment in the county jail is one year. The maximum fine is $1,000.

Shoplifting goods valued at $1,000 or more is a felony.

The maximum punishment in the Department of Corrections is five years. Voters approved a change to this statute on November 8, 2017 by passing SQ 780. The change went into effect on July 1, 2017.

SOURCE: 21 O.S. § 1731

Civil Liabilities That Are Implicated With A Shoplifting Charge

There are also civil liabilities that apply to shoplifting. These are covered by 21 O.S. § 1731.1. If you shoplifted, then you're liable in a civil action for either: 1) the retail price of the merchandise if it is unsalable or 2) the percentage of the diminished value of the merchandise due to the conversion—together with attorney fees and court costs.

The parent or legal guardian having custody of an unemancipated minor who shoplifts is liable in a civil action for either: 1) the retail price of the merchandise if it is unsalable or 2) the percentage of the diminished value of the merchandise due to the conversion—plus attorney fees and court costs.

An adult, emancipated minor, or unemancipated minor against whom judgment is rendered for shoplifting may also be required to pay exemplary damages. In lieu of the exemplary damages, any adult, emancipated minor, or unemancipated minor against whom a judgment for exemplary damages has been rendered may be required to perform public services designated by the court.

The provisions of the shoplifting statute are in addition to criminal penalties and other civil remedies. There is limitation on merchants or other persons from electing to pursue criminal penalties and other civil remedies, so long as a double recovery does not result. The law does not limit merchants from pursuing both civil and criminal remedies. You can be charged by both the state as well as have a pending civil case by the merchant; however, the merchant will not be entitled to no more than the amount that was stolen. If the merchant wins in civil court and you are also ordered to pay restitution by the criminal court, then you will only have to pay the merchant up to the value of the goods you shoplifted. Note that you can win your criminal case yet still have to pay restitution. This is because the merchant can still go after you in civil court. The burden of proof is much lower in a civil court than it is in a criminal court. The civil action for this must commence within two years after the violation occurred.

SOURCE: 21 O.S. § 1731.1

Oklahoma has several statutes that cover the theft or unlawful use of motor vehicles. The most common are Theft of Aircraft, Automobile, Automotive Driven Vehicle, or Construction or Farm Equipment; Unlawful Use of a Motor Vehicle; and Joyriding.

Theft Of Aircraft, Automobile, Automotive Driven Vehicle, Or Construction Or Farm Equipment

It's a felony to steal an aircraft, automobile or other automotive driven vehicle, construction equipment, or farm equipment. The range of punishment in the Department of Corrections is 3–20 years. The maximum fine is an amount that is equal to three times the value of the property that was stolen but no more than $500,000. Restitution must be paid.

SOURCE: 21 O.S. § 1720

Unauthorized Use Of Vehicle Or Implement Of Husbandry

It's a felony for a person who is not entitled to possession of a vehicle or implement of husbandry, without the consent of the owner and with intent to deprive the owner, temporarily or otherwise, of the vehicle or implement of husbandry or its possession, to take, use or drive the vehicle or implement of husbandry.

SOURCE: 47 O.S. § 4-102

Joyriding

A violation of this law occurs when someone loiters in or upon any automobile or motor vehicle; defaces or injures an automobile or motor vehicle; molests, drives, or attempts to drive any automobile, for joyriding or any other purpose; or manipulates or meddles with any machinery or appliances thereof without the consent of the owner of the automobile or motor vehicle.

This crime is a misdemeanor. The maximum punishment in the county jail is one year. The range of fine is $100–$500.

SOURCES: 21 O.S. § 1787 & 21 O.S. § 1788

Recent Changes To Theft Laws In Oklahoma

Oklahoma changed numerous theft laws between November 1, 2016 and July 1, 2017.

Changes Due To House Bill 2751

HB 2751 raised the threshold for a felony on many property crimes from $500 to $1,000. It affected the following laws:

- 21 O.S. 1451 – Embezzlement
- 21 O.S. 1521 – Motor Vehicle Lease or Rental - Payment by False or Bogus Check – Penalties
- 21 O.S. 1533.1 – Fraudulently Obtaining Personal Identity of Other Persons
- 21 O.S. 1541.1 – Obtaining Property by Trick or Deception - Attempt - False Representation or Pretense - Confidence Game – Penalty
- 21 O.S. 1541.2 – Penalty - Value of Property, Money, or Valuable Thing
- 21 O.S. 1541.3 – False or Bogus Checks, Drafts, or Orders – Penalty
- 21 O.S. 1542 – Obtaining Signature or Property by False Pretenses – Penalty
- 21 O.S. 1550.27 – False Making or Embossing of Credit

or Debit Card

- 21 O.S. 1550.32 – Receiving of Money, Goods or Services in Violation of § 1550.29 – Penalties
- 21 O.S. 1550.33 – Penalties for violation of Oklahoma Credit Card Crime Act
- 21 O.S. 1577 – Sale, Delivery or Receipt of Forged Notes or Instruments - Aggregation of Offenses Due to Formulation of Plan
- 21 O.S. 1578 – Possession of Forged Notes or Instruments - Aggregation of Offenses Due to Formulation of Plan
- 21 O.S. 1579 – Other Forged Instruments
- 21 O.S. 1592 – Publishing Counterfeited Instruments or Coins as True - Aggregation of Offenses Due to Formulation of Plan
- 21 O.S. 1621 – Penalty for Forgery - First Degree - Second Degree - Third Degree
- 21 O.S. 1704 – Grand Larceny and Petit Larceny – Definitions
- 21 O.S. 1705 – Grand Larceny – Penalty
- 21 O.S. 1731 – Larceny of Merchandise from Retailer or Wholesaler - Punishment - Subsequent Convictions
- 21 O.S. 1834 – Chattels Encumbered by Mortgage, Conditional Sales Contract or Security Agreement-Removal or Destruction

Changes Due To State Question 780

On November 8, 2016, Oklahoma voters again changed many property crime laws by passing SQ 780. Many of the statutes affected by SQ 780 were already changed by HB 2751. For the statutes that both HB 2751 and SQ 780 changed, the primary change was just the wording of the statutes. The effect of both was essentially the same. The changes from SQ 780 went into effect on July 1, 2017. SQ 780 changed the following statutes:

- 21 O.S. § 1704 – Grand Larceny and Petit Larceny – Definitions (previously changed by HB 2751)
- 21 O.S. § 1705 – Grand Larceny – Penalty (previously changed by HB 2751)
- 21 O.S. § 1713 – Receiving Stolen Property - Reasonable Inquiry Required
- 21 O.S. § 1719.1 – Larceny of Domesticated Fish and Game
- 21 O.S. § 1722 – Taking Oil, Gas, Gasoline - Misdemeanor - Felony
- 21 O.S. § 1731 – Larceny of Merchandise from Retailer or Wholesaler - Punishment - Subsequent Convictions (previously changed by HB 2751)
- 21 O.S. § 1451 – Embezzlement (previously changed by HB 2751)
- 21 O.S. § 1503 – Defrauding Hotels, Inns, Restaurants,

etc.

- 21 O.S. § 1521 – Motor Vehicle Lease or Rental - Payment by False or Bogus Check – Penalties (previously changed by HB 2751)
- 21 O.S. § 1541.1 – Obtaining Property by Trick or Deception - Attempt - False Representation or Pretense - Confidence Game – Penalty (previously changed by HB 2751)
- 21 O.S. § 1541.2 – Penalty - Value of Property, Money, or Valuable Thing (previously changed by HB 2751)
- 21 O.S. § 1541.3 – False or Bogus Checks, Drafts, or Orders – Penalty (previously changed by HB 2751)
- 59 O.S. § 1512 – Administration and Enforcement of Oklahoma Pawnshop Act
- 21 O.S. § 1577 – Sale, Delivery or Receipt of Forged Notes or Instruments - Aggregation of Offenses Due to Formulation of Plan (previously changed by HB 2751)
- 21 O.S. § 1578 – Possession of Forged Notes or Instruments - Aggregation of Offenses Due to Formulation of Plan (previously changed by HB 2751)
- 21 O.S. § 1579 – Other Forged Instruments (previously changed by HB 2751)
- 21 O.S. § 1621 – Penalty for Forgery - First Degree - Second Degree - Third Degree (previously changed by HB 2751)
- 21 O.S. § 51.3 was REPEALED - Punishment for Second and Subsequent Offenses after Conviction of Offense Punishable by Imprisonment in State

Penitentiary - Petit Larceny

The law that applies to a charge is the law that was in effect on the day of the offense. Therefore, for the crimes that both HB 2751 and SQ 780 changed, the wording of HB 2751 applies only if the offense was committed between October 31, 2016 and July 1, 2017.

SOURCES: HB 2751 & SQ 780

Potential Future Changes To Theft Laws In Oklahoma

Some Oklahoma legislators wanted to continue with the criminal justice reforms started by HB 2751 and SQ 780. However, the bill to increase the felony threshold on more property crimes was held up by opponents of criminal justice reform in 2017. HB 2281 would have changed the following statutes:

- 21 O.S. § 1416 – Delivery of Merchandise for Which Bill of Lading Issued - Exception
- 21 O.S. § 1451 – Embezzlement (previously changed by SQ 780)
- 21 O.S. § 1532 – False Personation - Receiving Money or Property Intended for Another
- 21 O.S. § 1541.2 – Penalty - Value of Property, Money, or Valuable Thing (previously changed by SQ 780)
- 21 O.S. § 1541.3 – False or Bogus Checks, Drafts, or Orders – Penalty (previously changed by SQ 780)
- 21 O.S. § 1577 – Sale, Delivery or Receipt of Forged Notes or Instruments - Aggregation of Offenses Due to Formulation of Plan (previously changed by SQ 780)
- 21 O.S. § 1578 – Possession of Forged Notes or Instruments - Aggregation of Offenses Due to Formulation of Plan (previously changed by SQ 780)
- 21 O.S. § 1579 – Other Forged Instruments (previously

changed by SQ 780)

- 21 O.S. § 1592 – Publishing Counterfeited Instruments or Coins as True - Aggregation of Offenses Due to Formulation of Plan (previously changed by HB 2751)
- 21 O.S. § 1702 – Larceny - Lost Property
- 21 O.S. § 1704 – Grand Larceny and Petit Larceny – Definitions (previously changed by SQ 780)
- 21 O.S. § 1705 – Grand Larceny – Penalty (previously changed by SQ 780)
- 21 O.S. § 1713 – (previously changed by SQ 780)
- 21 O.S. § 1720 – Theft of Aircraft, Automobile, Automotive Driven Vehicle, or Construction or Farm Equipment
- 21 O.S. § 1731 – Larceny of Merchandise from Retailer or Wholesaler - Punishment - Subsequent Convictions (previously changed by SQ 780)
- 47 O.S. § 4-102 – Unauthorized Use of Vehicle or Implement of Husbandry
- 47 O.S. § 4-103 – Receiving or Disposing of a Vehicle or Implement of Husbandry
- 47 O.S. § 17-102 – Penalties for Violations of The Uniform Vehicle Code
- 59 O.S. § 1512 – Administration and Enforcement of Oklahoma Pawnshop Act (previously changed by SQ 780)

This bill does many things. First, it rewrites some of the language changed in SQ 780 to have it conform to the style used in other statutes. This does not generally impact the result of the statute. It also adds tiers to some of the offenses. Where SQ 780 classified offenses as merely felonies and misdemeanors with two ranges of punishment, this bill adds multiple tiers of punishment for thefts greater than $1,000. In a few instances, this bill increases the maximum punishments for very high-value property. The general theme of this bill is in accordance with spirit of SQ 780, which is to reduce punishments for property crimes in Oklahoma. While this bill did not get enacted in 2017, it could be brought up again in 2018 and enacted.

SOURCE: HB 2281

Long-Term Effects Of Theft Charges On Someone's Record

Theft charges can have a huge long-term impact on somebody's record. This is because theft is considered a crime of moral turpitude. A crime of moral turpitude is,

generally, conduct that is considered contrary to community standards of justice, honesty, or good morals. If you have a conviction for a crime of moral turpitude, then you will have a very difficult time getting a job that deals with money or other people's property. You need to be very careful that you don't have any convictions or any sort of record for crimes of moral turpitude.

You want to think extra hard when pleading to a deferred sentence for a theft crime. If you don't think you will be able to abide by the terms, then they're going to haul you back into court and put a conviction on your record. You want to be very careful with crimes of moral turpitude because many good jobs involve handling money. You don't want to eliminate yourself from a wide variety of jobs that could be very beneficial to you. But, if you get a deferred sentence and complete the probationary terms, then you can potentially get that case expunged after it is dismissed.

What Should People Be Aware Of When Facing Theft Charges?

If your case cannot be dismissed, then expect to pay back whatever you took. Once you hire an attorney and you are paying your attorney, make sure you have a job to not only pay your attorney but to pay the restitution. If you have a plea deal, then you will also have to pay fines and court costs. There's going to be a lot of money involved, so you need to start working right away if you don't have a job. If you already have one job, then you'll likely need to get another one so you can have money to start paying things off now and prepare for paying more in the future.

DEFENDING THEFT CRIMES

The biggest thing to keep in mind with theft crimes is that money talks when trying to resolve your case. This means that restitution will often be the biggest issue in determining how good your outcome is. If you actually took what you're accused of taking and it wasn't yours, then it's more difficult to defend the charge. However, there are many defenses that can be used in theft cases. These are the following:

- You owned the property
- You mistakenly took the property
- You didn't have the intent to deprive another of the property you took
- Mistaken identification—someone else took the property, but you're the suspect
- Lack of evidence to prove that you took it
- You forgot to return something you borrowed
- Entrapment
- Intoxicated
- Owner consented to the taking
- Duress
- You believed you owned the property, but your good-faith belief was wrong

- You didn't take the property

There are also other defenses specific to the narrower theft crimes.

Oklahoma breaks burglary down into Burglary in the First Degree and Burglary in the Second Degree. Burglary will always be a felony charge. The punishments vary based on the type of burglary.

Different Levels Of Burglary In Oklahoma

Burglary in the First Degree is defined in 21 O.S. § 1431 as breaking into and entering the dwelling house of another, in which there is at the time some human being, with intent to commit some crime therein, either: 1) by forcibly bursting or breaking the wall, or an outer door, window, or shutter of a window of such house or the lock or bolts of such door, or the fastening of such window or shutter; 2) by breaking in any other manner, being armed with a dangerous weapon or being assisted or aided by one or more confederates then actually present; or 3) by unlocking an outer door by means of false keys or by picking the lock thereof, or by lifting a latch or opening a window.

Burglary in the Second Degree is defined in 21 O.S. § 1435

as breaking and entering any building or any part of any building, room, booth, tent, railroad car, automobile, truck, trailer, vessel, or other structure or erection, in which any property is kept, or breaking into or forcibly opening any coin operated or vending machine or device with intent to steal any property therein or to commit any felony.

How Intent Affects Burglary Charges

Intent is a very important element in a burglary charge because burglary is a specific intent crime. There are a couple of things to keep in mind here. First, the individual accused of burglary must have intended to commit a crime inside the structure prior to entering it. Somebody should not be found guilty who broke into a building then subsequently decided to commit a crime. The intent to commit a crime has to be formed prior to the breaking and entering. Being a specific intent crime, the mental state element can be negated through both voluntary and involuntary intoxication defenses.

In order to use the defense of voluntary intoxication, the individual has to be so intoxicated that they could not have formed the required intent to commit a crime prior to breaking and entering. Of course, the same applies to involuntary intoxication. However, voluntary intoxication is not a defense for committing a crime. It can only bring down the charge to a lesser-included offense that does not require a mental state of intent to commit a crime. So, if somebody in Oklahoma is so intoxicated that they could not form the intent to commit a crime prior to entering the building, the person could still be held liable for Breaking and Entering Without Permission, which is covered in 21 O.S. § 1438.

A burglary conviction should not result if the person willfully and intentionally broke into and entered a building without the owner's or occupant's permission but without the intent to commit a crime inside. For example, a person breaks into a house just to go to sleep. There is no intent to commit a crime inside, so that person should not be found guilty of burglary. On the other hand, somebody who does have the intent to commit a crime inside yet does not actually commit a crime inside can still be found guilty of burglary.

The facts surrounding the situation are going to dictate what the person's intent was. For example, if a person broke into a house and actually committed a crime inside, then it appears more likely that the person had the intent to commit a crime before they entered that house. If the person is found with implements of burglary, they are carrying a dangerous weapon, or they approach the victims in a threatening way, then that can also be evidence that they intended to commit a crime prior to entering the building.

Punishment For Burglary

21 O.S. § 1435 defines the punishment for burglary. The punishment range for Burglary in the First Degree is 7–20 years in the Department of Corrections. The punishment range for Burglary in the Second Degree is two–seven years in the Department of Corrections.

SOURCES: 21 O.S. § 1431, 21 O.S. § 1435, & 21 O.S. § 1436

POSSESSION OF IMPLEMENTS OF BURGLARY

The law covering possession of implements of burglary is 21 O.S. § 1437. This crime is a misdemeanor. It's illegal for someone who, under circumstances not amounting to a felony, has in his or her possession any dangerous offensive weapon or instrument whatever, or any pick-lock, crow, key, bit, jack, jimmy, nippers, pick, betty, or other implement of burglary, with intent to break and enter any building or part of any building, booth, tent, railroad car, vessel, or other structure or erection and to commit any felony inside of it.

The maximum punishment in the county jail is one year. The maximum fine is $500.

SOURCE: 21 O.S. § 1437 & 21 O.S. § 10

Factors That Can Enhance Or Aggravate A Burglary Charge

The manner by which the burglary is conducted or the target of the burglary can enhance a burglary charge. Burglary With Explosives and Burglary of a Controlled Drug are two examples of this.

Burglary With Explosives

Burglary With Explosives is covered in 21 O.S. § 1441. The use of explosives to enter certain structures or the use of explosives to open something inside the structure with explosives enhances a burglary charge. The minimum punishment in the Department of Corrections for Burglary With Explosives is 20 years.

Burglary Of A Controlled Dangerous Substance

The statute that covers Burglary, Larceny, or Theft of a Controlled Drug is 63 O.S. § 2-403. The maximum punishment in the Department of Corrections is ten years.

Effect Of An Injury During The Commission Of A Burglary

If there is an injury during the commission of a burglary or robbery, then the individual who caused the injury will pick up additional charges related to that injury. These can include Assault & Battery, Assault and Battery With a Dangerous or Deadly Weapon, or even Murder. These results can provide circumstantial evidence that the person intended to commit a crime inside, which would increase the chances of being found guilty of burglary. Somebody who burglarizes a house and injures somebody inside will likely be charged with both burglary and the crime related to the injury that the victim sustained.

SOURCES:

21 O.S. § 2-403, 21 O.S. § 1438, 21 O.S. § 1441, OUJI-CR 8-36, OUJI-CR 8-37, & OUJI-CR 8-38

WHAT DEFENSE STRATEGIES CAN BE USED IN BURGLARY CASES?

The first step is to look at the elements of the crime. There is a mental state and an act that must be performed. The mental state of intending to commit some crime inside must occur prior to the breaking and entering. The evidence has to be examined to determine if the prosecutor can prove beyond a reasonable doubt that the defendant intended to commit a crime inside prior to entering and if the defendant had the mental capacity to form that specific intent to commit the crime. Next, look at whether the wall, outer door, window, or shutter was forcibly opened. The defendant must have then entered somehow by breaking the plane of the door, window, shutter, etc.

Other defense strategies include:

- Didn't do it
- Lack of evidence
- Had the permission of the owner/occupier of the place you entered
- Thought you had the permission of the owner/occupier of the place you entered

- Intoxicated
- Entrapment
- Didn't have the intent to commit a crime inside
- The place entered doesn't meet the statutory definition of the place required to be entered
- Mistaken identification
- Coercion
- Duress

BREAKING AND ENTERING & ENTERING WITH THE INTENT TO COMMIT A FELONY

It is possible to be convicted for a couple of crimes that are similar to, but fall short of, burglary. These are Entering With the Intent to Commit a Felony and Breaking and Entering Without Permission.

Entering With The Intent To Commit A Felony

It is illegal to, under circumstances not amounting to any burglary, enter any building or part of any building, booth, tent, warehouse, railroad car, vessel, or other structure or erection with intent to commit any felony, larceny, or malicious mischief.

Breaking And Entering Without Permission

It is illegal to, without the intention to commit any crime therein, willfully and intentionally break and enter into any building, trailer, vessel or other premises used as a dwelling without the permission of the owner or occupant thereof, except in the cases and manner allowed by law.

Both of these crimes are misdemeanors. The maximum punishment in the county jail is one year. The maximum fine is $500.

SOURCE: 21 O.S. § 1438 & 21 O.S. § 10

What Is Robbery In Oklahoma?

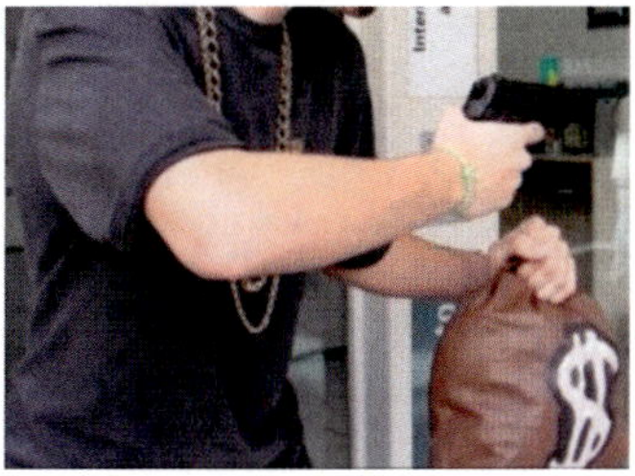

Robbery is defined in 21 O.S. § 791 as the wrongful taking of personal property in the possession of another, from his person or immediate presence, and against his will, accomplished by means of force or fear.

Force Component

When force is employed either to obtain or retain possession of the property, or to prevent or overcome resistance to the taking, then the degree of force employed does not matter. If force or fear is employed as a means of escape, then it does not constitute robbery.

Fear Component

Fear must also be employed either to obtain or retain possession of the property, or to prevent or overcome resistance to the taking. The fear that constitutes robbery may be either: 1) the fear of an unlawful injury, immediate or future, to the person or property of the person robbed or of any relative of his, or member of his family; or 2) the fear of an immediate and unlawful injury to the person or property of anyone in the company of the person robbed, at the time of the robbery.

Value Component

The value of the property involved in a robbery does not matter.

Knowledge Component

The taking of property from the person of another is not robbery when it clearly appears that the taking was fully completed without his or her knowledge.

Robbery In The First or Second Degree

The degrees of robbery are defined in 21 O.S. § 797. Robbery in the First Degree is when, in the course of committing the theft, the defendant: 1) inflicts serious bodily injury upon the person; 2) threatens a person with immediate serious bodily injury; 3) intentionally puts a person in fear of immediate serious bodily injury; or 4) commits or threatens to commit a felony upon the person. It is Robbery in the Second Degree when accomplished in any other manner.

Punishment For Robbery

The minimum punishment in the Department of Corrections for Robbery in the First Degree is ten years. The maximum punishment in the Department of Corrections for Robbery in the Second Degree is ten years.

SOURCES: 21 O.S. § 791, 21 O.S. § 792, 21 O.S. § 793, 21 O.S. § 794, 21 O.S. § 795, 21 O.S. § 796, 21 O.S. § 797, 21 O.S. § 798, & 21 O.S. § 799

Factors That Can Enhance Or Aggravate A Robbery Charge

A robbery charge can be aggravated by how the robbery was done. Robbery With a Dangerous Weapon or Imitation Firearm and Conjoint Robbery are examples of this.

Robbery With A Dangerous Weapon or Imitation Firearm

The statute that covers Robbery With a Dangerous Weapon or Imitation Firearm is 21 O.S. § 801. A person violates this statute when they rob or attempt to rob any person or persons, or if they rob or attempt to rob any place of business, residence or banking institution or any other place inhabited or attended by any person or persons with the use of any firearms or any other dangerous weapons. It doesn't matter whether the firearm is loaded or not. A violation of this law also occurs if the defendant uses a blank or imitation firearm capable of raising in the mind of the one threatened with such device a fear that it's a real firearm. The minimum

punishment in the Department of Corrections is five years.

Conjoint Robbery

The statute that covers Conjoint Robbery is 21 O.S. § 800. This occurs when two or more people work together to commit a robbery. The range of punishment in the Department of Corrections is 5–50 years.

Effect Of An Injury During The Commission Of A Robbery

If there is an injury during the commission of a robbery, then the individual who caused the injury will pick up additional charges related to that injury. These can include Assault & Battery, Assault and Battery With a Dangerous or Deadly Weapon, or Murder.

SOURCES: 21 O.S. § 800 & 21 O.S. § 801

DEFENSE STRATEGIES USED IN ROBBERY CASES

The first step in defending robbery charges is to look at the elements of the crime. Was the taking of personal property wrongful? Was it carried away? Was it from the immediate presence of another? Was the victim put in fear? Was the taking forceful?

Did the defendant threaten serious bodily injury? Did the defendant commit or threaten to commit a felony upon the victim?

Other defenses include:

- Didn't do it
- Intoxicated
- Entrapment
- Duress
- You actually owned the property
- Lack of evidence
- Victim never knew the property was taken
- Mistaken identity
- Coercion

Alternative Programs Available For First-Time Offenders

A defendant charged with theft, burglary, or robbery may plead to a deferred or suspended sentence. Deferred and suspended sentences consist of probation. The defendant receives an immediate conviction upon pleading to a suspended sentence. There is no immediate conviction when pleading to a deferred sentence. If the defendant successfully completes a deferred sentence, then the case will be dismissed.

Probation typically consists of restitution and classes. It's recommended that defendants get started on classes immediately. Prosecutors typically want to see the defendant attend classes that promote the cessation of behavior that brought on the charges. Taking the classes early can often help improve the plea offer.

Restitution will always be a part of any type of sentence, whether it's deferred or not. If you took the property and still have it, then you must give it back or pay for it. Returning the items and/or paying restitution early can also help improve the plea offer.

There are other options available to younger offenders. These include being deemed a Youthful Offender and Regimented Inmate Discipline.

Youthful Offender

Oklahoma's Youthful Offender (YO) Act allows teenagers charged with serious crimes the opportunity for release into the community if they complete a treatment program. Robbery and burglary are on the list of serious crimes that allow a juvenile to be eligible for YO status. Typical treatment includes therapy, continuing education, and not getting charged with new offenses. A juvenile 13–17 years old could be considered a YO.

A YO will begin his or her sentence as a juvenile in the juvenile system. The YO may then be transferred to the adult system when they turn 18. The YO can stay in the juvenile system until he or she is 20. If the YO is successful with their treatment program, then he or she could get released from custody when they turn 21. If the YO is not successful in the treatment program, then he or she will serve out the remainder of their sentence in the adult system.

SOURCE: 10A O.S. §§ 2-5-201–2-5-301

Regimented Inmate Discipline

Regimented Inmate Discipline (RID) is a deferred sentencing option for young adults who are neither youthful offenders nor juveniles. The defendant must be 18–21 years old at the time of their plea. RID is structured as a "boot camp" environment. It can last 180 days–one year. Some counties have an out-of-custody RID program.

The defendant must be accused of a non-violent felony to be eligible for RID, so a defendant charged with First Degree Robbery or First Degree Burglary would not be eligible for RID. Upon successful completion of RID, the court may defer the sentence, suspend the sentence, impose a sentence in the Department of Corrections, impose community sentencing, or dismiss the charges.

SOURCE: 22 O.S. §§ 996.1–996.3

Implications Of A Robbery Or Burglary Conviction In Oklahoma

It is very difficult for someone who committed any type of robbery or burglary to enter a diversion program. For example, drug court does not allow someone charged with a violent crime to enroll in the program. A robbery or burglary charge would have to be amended to something not as bad to even allow somebody to be eligible for drug court. However, that is very difficult because these are considered violent crimes. Prosecutors are not typically willing to accommodate people whom they feel have committed acts of violence. It is possible to get a deferred or suspended sentence on these charges. However, that would, in the vast majority of cases, likely only apply to a first-time offender.

Prosecutors will likely not be willing to offer a deferred or suspended sentence for these crimes, so another way to get a deferred or suspended sentence would be through a blind plea.

Blind Plea

A blind plea is essentially where the defendant throws himself or herself on the mercy of the court. Think of it like a mini trial. The defendant admits guilt and asks the judge for mercy. The prosecutor puts on their case as to why the defendant should receive the punishment they think the defendant deserves. Then, the defense has the opportunity to tell the court what they think the punishment should be. As defense attorneys, we hope that the judge sees our point of view better than the prosecutor's. This is a good time to present mitigating evidence that we may not have otherwise been able to bring up in trial, so it's a good idea to know a lot about the client's background and the good things they've done.

For instance, we can talk about the client's military service and their upbringing. Maybe they lived in a foster home and had a lot of negative influences, or maybe their parents were drug addicts. These are things that a defense attorney can use to humanize the client and hopefully get the judge to feel sympathy. A blind plea is a good thing to do when the offer from the prosecutor is bad, you don't think that going to a jury trial would yield a better outcome, and going to the judge might give you a better outcome than the previous two options.

85% Crimes

Oklahoma refers to some crimes as “85% crimes.” These crimes are listed in 21 O.S. § 13.1. They are considered the worst types of crimes that can be committed. Individuals convicted of these crimes are not eligible to earn any credits that have the effect of reducing the length of the sentence to less than 85% of the sentence imposed. If you’re convicted of Burglary in the First Degree or Robbery in the First Degree, then you will have to serve a minimum of 85% of your sentence.

SOURCES: 57 O.S. § 571 & 21 O.S. § 13.1

MILITARY & CHARGED WITH THEFT, BURGLARY, OR ROBBERY

A theft, burglary, or robbery charge can be devastating to a military career. In my 18+ years in the military, I have seen careers ended due to just being charged with a crime. If you get arrested for a crime, your career could effectively be over. You typically won't be allowed to promote or re-enlist. If you are ever charged with any theft, burglary, or robbery crime, then your odds of getting into the military are slim to none.

An issue that I see with members of the military, having been on active-duty for over ten years, is that members who get arrested are believed to be guilty just because they were arrested. Our system is supposed to presume people innocent until proven guilty. Unfortunately, that's not the case with many military unit commanders. What they typically do is try to make an example out of people.

Take an arrest that happens over the weekend as an example. The commander will find out about it and have the individual report in their service dress uniform early Monday morning. The commander will grill them about what happened. The member may even have to talk to several commanders about what happened. Additionally, the individual may have to stand before his or her peers and explain what happened. I've even seen a situation where the commander opened it up to questions from members of the audience. People in the audience were asking the arrestee questions! So, these are all things that members of the military can be subjected to—shame, embarrassment, and railroading.

The biggest problem here is the breakdown in the presumption of innocence. Therefore, I try as hard as I can to get across the importance of maintaining the presumption of innocence. If you go before your commander, then you can exercise your right to remain silent. You don't have to tell people what happened. What you say can and will be held against you—even though it's not to law enforcement. Once you tell one person, it's over. Let your attorney look over the evidence and discuss your case with you before you talk about it with anybody. You'll be threatened and made to feel bad, but just know that you have rights. Don't let higher-ranking people trample on those rights.

If you're in the military and you get arrested, you can be tried on or off base. If it's off base, then it will be handled by the state or city prosecutor. It's usually not transferred to the JAG office on base. However, that does happen sometimes. If you're arrested on base, then it's possible that your case will be prosecuted on base. The base's Area Defense Counsel (ADC) helps defend people on base. They're the public defenders for members of the military. You can certainly hire a private attorney to handle your case on base. You would want somebody who's familiar with the UCMJ, the Uniform Code of Military Justice, because that's the body of law that they'll be using to prosecute you.

If you're prosecuted off base, you want representation from someone who's familiar with the procedures and the law for whatever jurisdiction is prosecuting you. Therefore, the ADC will likely not be helping you if your case is prosecuted off base.

Another consequence that arrested members of the military face is an Article 15—known as "non-judicial punishment." Instead of going through a Court Martial, the commander can punish the member through an Article 15. This basically means that the commander can punish the member in some way. Instead of going through a Court Martial, they put pressure on the members to talk and implicate themselves. It's difficult to get out of it at that point.

The Article 15 is often the easiest way for the commander to go. The punishments can range from extra duty on the weekends to being confined to base—or even to getting kicked out. What often happens after a service member's arrest is that the punishment received through an Article 15 is something that makes the service member unpromotable, so they must separate when their time is up. The punishment varies based on the severity of the crime that the member is alleged to have committed.

When a soldier is accused of breaking the law, the Army issues a General Officer Memorandum of Reprimand (GOMOR). This is written by a General Officer reprimanding a soldier for their alleged bad behavior. The GOMOR can become part of the soldier's military files. If it's filed locally, then it will eventually be removed from the soldier's files. A GOMOR filed in the soldier's permanent file will likely stay there forever; this is devastating to a soldier's chances of staying in the Army. It's important for a soldier to do whatever is necessary to prevent the GOMOR from becoming a permanent part of his or her file.

If you had planned on making the military a career, then one lapse in judgment can end those dreams. So, it's very important to hire an attorney who understands what's going on with the military, the culture there, and what they're going to try to do to you. You must find an attorney who is going to do everything they can to obtain an outcome that's not going to end your career.

DEFINITIONS

ADC – Area Defense Counsel

ARIDE – Advanced Roadside Impaired Driving Enforcement

GOMOR – General Officer Memorandum of Reprimand

HB – House Bill

JAG – Judge Advocate General

O.S. – Oklahoma Statute

OSCN – Oklahoma State Court Network

RID – Regimented Inmate Discipline

SFST – Standardized Field Sobriety Test

SQ – State Question

UCMJ – Uniform Code of Military Discipline

YO – Youthful Offender

DISCLAIMER

This publication is intended to be informational only. No legal advice is being given, and no attorney-client relationship is intended to be created by reading this material. If you are facing legal issues, whether criminal or civil, seek professional legal counsel to get your questions answered. The law cited is current as of November 1, 2017. Laws are subject to change at any time.

THE URBANIC LAW FIRM, PLLC

1141 N Robinson Avenue
Suite 101
Oklahoma City, OK 73103
(405) 633-3420

Frank@Urbanic.Law

Made in United States
Orlando, FL
05 November 2026

90200570R10057